THE JOURNEY
Book of Poetry

BY

Shonita S. Stevenson

Isaiah 43:1-4
Isaiah 55:6
Proverbs 9:10
Psalm 96:9
Psalm 29:2
Psalm 112:7
Matthew 6:31
Matthew 19:26
Matthew 26:28
Colossians 3:1-2
Hebrews 11:1
Acts 3:19
Romans 3:23
Philippians 4:6
Philippians 4:13

Introduction

The journey is a book of poetry that tells a story of everyday struggles, patience, wisdom, faith, and victory in the Christian walk here on earth. The journey is not just Poetry, it's a book about life and it covers milestones of roads traveled short and far and yet, is remarkable in a strong message for today. It is spoken word written to speak to the heart and will minister hope. It is spoken word written to speak volumes to the spirit and soul of men and women.

The journey is different in retrospect, from most Christian based poems. The Journey opens to the open-heart and reveals God's work, working from the inside out. I believe this book will touch lives for the Kingdom of God to restore and renew in mind, body, and soul. It is poetry that stirs up the spirit; that believes there is hope, faith and victory in all parts of life.

The journey speaks volumes and yet shows the many facets of life on earth. I believe you will laugh, cry, and ponder on the many mysteries of God and what God will do in your life. I believe the joy that comes from reading parts of this book will touch your heart in such a special way. I have faith that you find the pleasure in reading this book, as I did in writing from my heart to yours. Enjoy!

Thank you,
Isaiah 43:1-4

Book Dedication

This book of poetry is dedicated to first the Lord, Jesus Christ. I want to thank you Lord for this gift, I want to thank you that, the Kingdom of Heaven is exalted on high. I dedicate this to Clarence Scott Jr. (Jazz Man) you were the sparkle in a little girl's eye. To grandma, I remember the white gloves and I have the bible you once held. To grand-dad, those grayish eyes and to my grand-mother I didn't know. I'll see you again one day. I Love you.

Acknowledgments

I want to thank my mom for her encouragement and vision for things that, I could not see and for knowing the Holy Spirit is always right. I appreciate you Mom for your insight and wisdom and for being my mother, I Love You. I want to thank my brother Clarence for allowing me to be your sister, I appreciate your zeal for the art of poetry and rap the other 'genre', I Love you.

To all my aunts and uncles whom I adore and love; each of you is significant in my life and has been always. I will always be "little Shonette". To wonderful friends over the span of my life; to Dr. Allen for listening even when it wasn't your favorite thing to do; however, your support and all the great pens is so appreciated. To Momma Bobbie and all the prayer warriors, thank you for your many prayers (I feel it!). I appreciate you all. It's just nice to know God is so awesome and prayer is the most powerful tool known to man.

Thank you,

Table of Contents

Introduction iv
Book Dedication v
Acknowledgments vi

Salvation
Grace 1
Who Is That Knocking? 2
Washed 3

Love / Betrayal / Forgiveness
Careful 5
Cast Upon Me 8
Cherished 9
Find You 10
Forsaken Identity 11
Ice… 12
It Is New 13
Justify 14
Love 15
Old Wounds … 17
The Game 19

Vision / Dreams
Across The Way 20
It Is Me… 21
See 22
It's Possible 23
Kaleidoscope 24
Moments 25
Reminiscence... 26
Visions 27
Writing Words.. 28

Faith / Words
Hope Floats.. 29
More Than Words 30
Reasons 31
Spoken 32

This Pen… 34
Words 35

Backslid / Pain / Struggle
Enough Cry 36
Repent I 37
Thoughts 38
Back Away 39
Crossroads 40
In The Crowd 41
No Fault Line 42
Procrastination 43
Quickness 44
Sand Trap 45
Twisted 46

Single
Age Tingles 47
Harmony 48
I Bet 49
Possibilities 51
Private Thoughts 52
Something Real 54
Who Will Love Her? 55

Happiness / Joy / Thanksgiving
Lovely 57
World's Finest 58
Writing Music 59
A Talk With God 60

Ministry
Calling 61
Inspire 62
Someone To Bless 63
Stage 64
The Way U Love Me 65
The Word Says I Can 66
Where Is My Friend? 67
Wisdom 68

Failure / Accomplishment / Success
Gifted Hands 69
Good Respect 71
No Vanity 72
The Champ 73
This Man 74
Well Done 75

Purpose
Quote 76
The Content Of My Character 77
Climate Change 78
You Are 79
Self-Check 81
Understand 82

Family / Mother's
A Bridge 83
Because 84
Brother 85
Grandmother 86
Hand To Mouth 88
Jazz Man 89
Uncle 90

Marriage
Soul Connected Christian 92
An Evening Affaire 94
I Bid To You, Anew And Fresh 95
Imagine That 97
Moonlight Bliss 100
Silhouette Of Love 101
Sum Love Come Stay 103

Praise and Worship
Clap 104
Flowing Rivers 105
Give Thanks 106
Grateful 107
Jubilee 108
Mimic Me Lord 109

Shout...111
Thankful..112
This Is The Time To Worship.....................................113

Humanity / Unity
My Brother..115
Planet Called Earth 116
Poets Unite...118
At Your Service...119
Symphony Of Life… 120
The Hour...121
The Latter 122
The Writing On The Wall...123
United 124
Where I Go 126
Vapors 127

Grace

Spirit to Spirit eyes do see and heart can hear – that Love is waiting here.
Waiting to show mercy and grace.
To calm the rocky and wavy sea
To bear the struggle over the mountain that appears high.
To hold the enemy by words that contains him.
To give grace where it can't be shown or seen to man.
To unravel the web of confusion that once mangled the mind from the impossible
And
Now knows the possible is candid.
To grasp grace like life that lives within

Grace

Carries power alone,
Shows her gentleness in soft ways.
Gives herself a fresh start everyday and administers patience,
In a lost forsaken place, giving and giving to the wounded, afflicted, battered, and tattered, torn and dismayed grace shows compassion without say.

Grace

Who is she?
Where did she come from?
Where does she reside?
How did she come to know this side?

Grace

Can be defined by the actions portrayed,
Grace is silent and relentless in time.
Inevitably, she earned her keep.
Grace never shows she is wearing thin,
She never shows malice or disgrace.
She just continues to give with Love by her side.

© 2008 April 21
Grace

Who is that knocking?

Hey, what you doin' here?
How did you get here... right here, Where I am right now?
Holy Spirit is knocking.

Did you just happen to see feet walkin' by?
Trying to feel the vibe in those steps.
Pacing edging on the future brink
Not rushing, not anxious, just want to see that God's got something,
God's up to somethin' and always is.

Hey, what's going on over here and over there can you see it is it really
happening right now? Can tell you any thing cause' cryin' louder than
hearing is all the same seeing things the way you do –
Don't think the door will open until the Holy Spirit arrives in you.

Wow, gettin' closer to this thing named calling.
Closer to destiny can't fall kind of bracing the wall for the jolt about to
rock the halls in places like in the soul causing blessings, blessing
coming down falling faster than one can pry coming, falling fast. So,
catch, catch.
Catch a few in your hand.

© 4-November-2009
 Knockin'

Washed

Caught in the circumvent crossed fate and made into a spectacle of circumstance.
Barreling down at 100 miles per hour in the slow lane at that,
Traded with an inside trader and displaced trust at the start.
Now, it's apart tangled in a web of motivated adrenaline gone wild.

Out-of-control sparked with a slight delight just right for the appetite,
Doing things grown folks shouldn't do… twisted and whisked away in lustful pleasure.
Mixed up in a confused state.

Tried washing out the dirt but, dirty stains too deep, slipping undercover,
in the face in shame and denial on trial with self-rushing to conclusion that, it's over it's through already forgot about you.

Crafty and cluttered in threes and four's thought there was a secret.

Never to scorn

Hugging and holding seemed so tight until more is in the light.
It was a game and the prey had become the frayed.
Given time to simmer it down, anger built up inside, just unwind need some time.

Cut, cut so deep into the heart that, the knife went all the way through.
Fragile is spelled differently in mind, subside holding onto the lie, so far inside.
How do you keep that poker face? The enemy is a lie.

But

Bottom line there is forgiveness. There is much to wash and cleansed.
The places the enemy tries to defeat from afar are places of lies in the ear trying to taint the spirit from coming around. So, one last look was all it took to realize your washed. Washed with grace, rinsed by the blood, restored by faith, no character disgrace.
So, look into the mirror and see fate.

Can you see it all?

You have been washed.

Matthew 26:28

©7-March-2010
Washed

Careful

I do not hate. I appreciate the time, the time spent just you and me.
Tried something different for a change in mind, didn't think I'd grow to
want to stay for awhile, away late nights ...all night.

A cocktail after two for two on a weekday rendezvous,
Order of the good for something platter of truth on the table
For your listening pleasure and in return... was the same I'd hope.

Mysterious concoction of figuring out clues came unglued,
Gave the story blues when all you had to do was ask.
Ask for the answers and the reason behind a distant lover.
Playing to allow peace of mind in time as time went flying by.
By, By, Bye.

Listening to this or that for a while drawing cumbersome to unreliable,
undeniable, and unequivocal matters, unappreciated, the real that was
underneath, hidden compartments in the deep of heart gave way to lies
and deceit or was it defeat?

Careful, careful not to stumble and fall, fall, and tumble.
Tumble down on face first, smashing to pieces dreams, desired in
thought.
Careful, to not explode on a dime because it was good having you
around.
Around and about, about in out sometimes just because.

Careful, not to stretch too far apart the truth, apart in a world unlike
most and to some that, never dare to touch or pry open with peeping
eyes so, as the story is told the story unfolds.
For the sake of crying, weeping eyes filled up with dreadful tears of
why?
No sadness.

A mystery to you and not to some and then again maybe, maybe it was
because the
Door was always cracked enough for me to see with eyes wide open
and ears too soft to really hear. A mystery to you and not to some and
then again maybe, maybe it was the too honest to believe that this could
be happening to you, something sweet.

*Careful, to see too deep into your spirit, the spirit man of painfulness
and thoughtlessness.*
*So, this is how it turned out to be? Is this how you wanted it to be? To
go far and away because it was too real to escape.*

*Gathering up my heart again and holding it open for the surreal,
becoming selective as an elective for the good at heart. Careful to not
look but, see inside the insider, the cleverness of heart defined by time
defined by gravity and frailty.*

*You put in twenty-two and got the best part of life sucked right out of
you.*
*Living life or letting the life live you. Not a clue. You could never see
what I could see in you.*

Careful

*Caution, danger, warning signs that flash right before eyes, seeing
visions of your moves on the board... in the night, shifting to swift... feet
that stammer towards Pandora's box cranking the arm to see it go pop,
pop, pop!*
Careful to be careful.

*It started with a clean slate and lead to fate and then a date, open me
up to you and
Laid some milestones before you, dusted it off and smiled at you; was
letting you know that I wasn't involved.*

Careful to be kind.

Careful

Whispers of spirit to ear inclined to hear, searching me to capture me.

*And then you became callous, cold, and clammy, unkind, discontent,
dishonest washed and wearing your feelings tattooed across your back,
as though you were martyr perplexed and fixed for truths untold.*

*You wanted to own want you did not work for and worked for less than
what you were willing to give though... oops my bad for thinking that I*

could change a battered, tattered, small minded little boy into an overnight success.

It just does not work that way, I guess!

Careful, to be careful and not enough for you.

Careful to be giving of a heart that, was kind and true
But, then again, look who rescued you.

©July 20, 2009
Careful

Cast Upon Me

The benevolent rays of life and
Show ways that are sweet and kind.

True are the words softly spoken with of conviction and courage rocking
swift?
Like a lullaby... soothing the mind to rest
Gently,

Cast upon me...

Fate and in time, time will take care of itself.
Or not
Show thy way pure.
And
In a moment's cares,
The heart will grow fonder, full of love, gentle.
Calming reasons to give real-ness.

Cast upon me...

Thy love and do not forsake.
Surely the rain comes, and it falls quickly down in quiet, still and subtle
miles.

Cast upon me...

Happiness, joy, laughter and thus forget.
Where the thrust of the journey lies.

Enjoying the earthly realm called, Life?

Or not...it is temporal, least and most forgot.

© 2/11/09
Revised
Cast upon me

Cherished

Moments are here today and gone tomorrow.

Yet, the memories live on imbedded within.

Within these walls, corridors traveled walking down these halls,

Feeling the good and separating the falls.

Cherished...

Yesterday is and tomorrow is last.
Waiting to grasp, the now.

To embrace time, time that waits no longer.
Skipping through these, stopping, and listening to sound,
Lost in translation and restored, tomorrow waits, and waits no more.

Taking the chance to live, laugh and smile...

Deep breathes... deep breathes and ... hold.

Holding back the tears of now

Cherish ...

Cherish and savor the taste of life.

©December 22, 2009
Cherished

Find You

It has taken me a lifetime to find you,

Going thru cities and tearing down walls.

It's taken me a lifetime to find you and not fall.

Going thru towns, crossing high seas, landing on seashores in distant lands afar

And

Yet the search has cost me a price to pay,

Never having that which has taken away ...

I have waited this long, and a moment longer will not starve this destiny until destiny has her way and alas, I find treasure in stones that no man takes.

I find you.

I find you again.

I find Love.

It's taken me a lifetime to find you,
Going thru lost valleys and tossing out caravans of weight that held me down.
Now, I found you.
Now, I find you again.
Now, I find Love.

© 21-June-2010
Find You

Forsaken Identity

If eye to eye is where we do not meet, it does not mean a possible defeat.

And just because friends take great test; it does not mean less.

I will care just the same as I did before we were friends.

But,

The road is rough and now you don't know me at all.

I do forgive and I apologize for it all.

Just the same…

©*7/14/1989*
Forsaken Identity

ICE...

Complicated enough to explain the complexity of this thang,
This thang, wreckin' this flow like when you left the show, lights dimmed
out, turned off.

Caving in like an avalanche high in the mountains,
Like ice capades show flow,
Thawing out to your words, coming to,
Coming through, cold ice piece
Sculptured by raw hands.
Set it on chill for a while, waiting for the flavor to settle in
In like Lawry's seasoning.

Complicated enough to let go,
Feelin' like calling a tow, pulling this weight,
Place it on freight.

Going, going ... gone like. Thinking you played when you got' played,
On stage ... listening to a hint of laughter when you are exiting.
Snickering in the back, watching your back,
Ice ... cold.

Craving out a new box. Pandora ain't got this part,
A start into a Separating heart,
Cold ice ... shot in a glass.

Tried to instill meaning to what it is and what it was.
Ice cold, Stone cold, can't compare to the, scribbled up on pause. Think
it shall be called, Absalom!

You in spirit is Ice.

© 6.24.2010
Ice

It is New

Words spill onto paper like water to the floor.

I know you are Lord.

The sense of knowing fills my spirit so, so much that, I can't retain the tears that flow.

Filling eyes, much to be joyous about ... my heart is elated.

And related to you Oh God above! So, that I shout! Shout!

To know destiny is the life you gave me, I can not refrain.

I belong to you Oh Lord.

Relentless in commitment to your word,

Tells me the Love you have for me is greater than I know.

©March 3, 2009
It's new

Justify

Justify love.

Justify what it does.

Justify how it cares.

How it sustains and how it maintains.

Justify its purpose,

And show how it grows…only Heaven knows.

Justify the meaning.

Justify the feeling.

Justify the sadness.

Justify the moods and how it removes,

Justify its reason.

And show how it transforms.

Justify what can't be justified.

Love has a meaning to why it cares,

How it dares to sustain and maintain throughout the years, its purpose is valid in what is felt emotionally.

But, more importantly it has transformed a reason into believing.

How it's justified by love.

© July 22, 2009
Justify

L   O   V   E

The quest for this thing called love is indoctrinating, intoxicating.
Embedded into DNA fibers of the soul crushing all possibilities that
love can not and will not have control.

One thing about love is that love has traveled before mankind.
It was love that created the fabric of being.
Embroidered a lifetime mark into the heart,
Gave longing its first start.

This thing about love it has endless boundaries beyond
understanding.
Beyond trying to deny it love has dominated and ruled kings, queens,
and kingdoms.
Dictated forgiveness by stretching out love hands to render surrender.
Love.

The quest for this thing called love is intriguing, fascinating, and
mysterious.
Embedded into the core fibers of souls and boundaries.
It is, what it is, this love.

Deniably true and forever told in books, poems, songs, and speeches;
it reins to
Be supreme over all others that dare conquer her, she sits with
wisdom and hold hands with hope, she gives faith its own seat to
dance with her.
None compete nor can defeat loves power to sustain.

This thing about love is that love has countless fans jamming isles,
courts, beaches of sand, standing on land, singing loudly, ringing
vigorously demanding a look and not a glance, she is woven into the
fine streamed lines of life.

Without her, something would seize to exist, without knowing what she
endured,
She keeps her end of the bargain, she's always willing and never
compromise.

And

How do I know this about love?

Because she loaned it to me when I did not know her at all.

©1-March -2010
Love

Old wounds ...

Old wounds must heal with time.
And
Time can only make it subside.

In the moment when less is thought,
Another brings back the wrought that fought.
A challenge for the mind to conceive the hateful thoughts of deceit can
only make one.

Old wounds that must heal and will heal in time.
And
Time can only make them subside.
In a moment or less when few words cause stress,
One will arise and triumph with arms outstretched.
Giving glory to the God above!

Old wounds that lapsed in the night held in the light.
For all to see and all to hear, there goes the fight.
In the moment when the mess is less and the smile returns,
Knowing that God is renewing the laughter again, and the smile again.

Old wounds that will fade and never to be made.
Who will sing a song, who will sing praise?
Oh! God our redeemer heals our lives with your spirit and make anew.
Change us in an instant that we are new and live without timidity.

Old wounds go away, go away from here and never to return.
The road at this time has traveled rough and jagged edges have cut skin
and bled much, tears rough, become frayed and laid to die, to rest,
fixing the heart, fixing the hurt, fixing all that is within... to forgive and
let live.

Old wounds, where there is no control of loose lips and ringing ears.
Let us hear the word of God, fill in our souls with truth and not despair.
Give me oh God a sensitive heart, pure and strong to continue this walk.
Not to stalk in the night, to rest and close these heavy eyes.

Old wounds are no more and must be not.
Comprise nor compromise. But be it not DENIED.

© 3-February-2010
Old wounds

The Game

Who dares to see with eyes shut?
Who dares to walk with no strut?

Leaving behind a word that can be wise or can devise ... in the game.

One who dares to see without touch, is plainly and simply abrupt.

It is one who does not hear and knowing they have eyes is only to deny.

And willing to play the game.

But, not willing to lose the game.

© 11/18/1985
The Game

Across the Way

There is a lady across the way, she is staring a mile away.
She rocks in an old rocking chair, whistling in the wind in God's song.

Across the way there she sits and waits.
Rocking on memories by the lake.
The lake between the homes where the ducks swam, and the geese flocked.

Across the way, she watches the boats go by and children play on the slides.
The water sways, the currant frays, the sun fades in orange and reds.
Across the way, she sits and stares, remembering beauty of the pictures past once hanging high.

Across the way, she smiles, she laughs, and she reminisce. She wonders. Just how fast the time flies by as she watches the tide and how it's gone by .. as she closes her eyes.

© August 4, 1993
Revised 10.23.09
Across the way

It is me...

Lord It is me.
I had a better day than yesterday.
Because you're doing for me what I wouldn't be able to do for myself,
which is to
Cleanse me,
Heal me,
Restore me,
Hold me,
And
Love me.

You Lord is the greatest thing.
You Lord made my day,
You loved me when I woke up,
You cared enough to breathe the breath of life in me.

This day Lord was another victory and another day for me to be a living
testimony with my presence, with my life.

You Lord is inevitable.
You are countless in measure and purer than the purest element, created
by you!

Lord, I love you.

It's me Lord.

I thank you.

© 4/28/99
It's me

See

I see there is an opening where no one else can see.
I see the door is thinning in between the cracks of the seam.
I see the passage is much like a running stream, something like,
Parallels of congruent themes,
I am exemplifying dreams.

I see faith exposed composed of poems,
I see where God has found me poised, something like,
Waterfalls at noon, pouring into my spirit, make room.

A greater knowledge then every known,
I see hope in a newfound strength, more encouraging.
I see the canals of panama from a mountain high and clouds are my
wings that carries me farther into De Janeiro finding the serenity under
the redeemers' arms outstretched over all of Rio.

I see the manifestation taking place,
I see purpose given and gained during rebirth, relentless and futile.
I see change happening right now,
Where you will find me... is in him.
The Lord our God in all his reproof, refined, alive and renewed.

©4/29/2009
Revised 12/23/09
I see

It's Possible

It's possible to Live and Love with arms opened wide.
Flourishing to the highest level of all that's within,
A promise of feeling less lonely than before.

Learning to compromise beyond an understanding that's intended for those that have been doing it a lot longer.

It is possible.
It's possible to learn and laugh at the same time because mistakes happen.
Captivating and emerging to another elevated level of all that's within a knowing of, feeling more than before, teaching to understand beyond the point of letting wisdom, guide for the ones that don't mind becoming intuitive.

It's possible because anything is possible with believing and having the faith that conquers all, a faith that is stronger than just believing more than before, giving the gift within, to be able to receive all that has been given.

It's possible that all that exist is because of order in relationship.
Relationship that is intended to create obedience and integrity,
A hope of these things known stand as a test to the will of life as we know.

Anything and everything are possible.
Possible to encourage realism that love survives through the test of time and without it; there is no compassion for life to produce new life into existence.

So, dare all the possible aspects that are good to form its creativity into being by words that speak faith and life…

And

Live.

The impossible, is possible!

© *July 30, 2009*
It's possible

Kaleidoscope

Changin' right in front of me.
Kinda' like you are feelin' me.
Colorless until it lands, lands on shades of multi-colored sand.
Kaleidoscope of rare condition,
Drivin' not to catch any emissions into my Nostrils.

Kaleidoscope.

Changin' me, reforming me into matter, that's solid.
Quiet in-lays of sweet reminiscing words resting on ears that,
Want to hear something, something kind and subtle.
Spin it again, spin it.
Catching parallels of colors intertwine to refine,
This state of mind
Bout' feelins'.
Kaleidoscope of consistency.
Kaleidoscope of backgrounds.

Someone put the cap on the paint that's spilling frowns.
An array of majestic, mosaic art in motion
Gathering to see

Kaleidoscope...

©September 23, 2009
Kaleidoscope

Moments

Moments like this make me feel moments.
This could be something I've wanted all my days.
Moments like this make life worth more the living.
I mean it's just the way God makes us… right?

The essence of life exists because of God and now I know it's his love that surrounds me wherever I am.
Moments like this, makes me reach way down, down, down… inside to grab a piece of my mind, heart, and soul, staying' here for love, praying to go home one day.

It hasn't destroyed me, just made me stronger and stronger to live and gain, search and love more more of me and yeah; me and my God, family and just.

These moments…

Like the one I'm having and telling you all in one breathe that it's okay – we all hurt, trying to guess at something that we've been in search of and finding it and losing it and then picking it back up to start all over again.

Love ….

Some of us just don't give anymore, to know what it's like, you know that Love people give up on … cause Love never changes its form… it's the people that we choose to Love… so just forgive.

Moments, like this make me smile to be a child of God… because he chose me to Love in this time, in this place, on this earth within the inhabitants of this world for his time.
We yearn to understand with great understanding, with compassion and hope.

Moments like this are sacred and I just wanted to share this moment with you.

© May 6, 2008
Moments

Reminiscence on this day.
A day to remember the value of our lives.
One day we will acknowledge our sorrows and our good-byes.
Tomorrow rejoices for that day we look forward to...
And
The next day we will see how it goes.

But, tonight, sit quietly and listen with a heart of truth.
And
Complete what is started and call a truce for angered words said.
And
Rest ourselves with a certain simplicity that, would seem like the right thing to do.

©*2/27/1990*
Reminiscence

Visions

I'm listening to silence in bed.
Cannot sleep with things in my head.
Rolled over bout' ten times.
Trying to switch sides.
Imagining my eyes open then shut,
Clutter, click and cluck. I think I'm stuck.

Seeing stars in the night against the ceiling so bright.
Feeling, I'm starting to see visions, am I dreaming?
In the night, of images of past and present sights,
Slow blink, slow wink, goes my eyes, feeling like I spy.
In the middle of the night, patterns aligned for future,
Events, my hands are in cement, pulling apart sections of unraveled
scenes of real people, places, and things.

Visions of imaginable and the unimaginable happening to,
Many in different places and yet the same comes true.
There goes my eye, winking then blinking to keep the night dust from
leaking on to me.

I'm seeing visions come and go, go and come.
Vividly surreal in a moments rush, adrenaline flush to full thrust,
Roaring into spiritual gates of fourth dimensions stuff, factoring
through warring territories of a different kind.
Finding the secrets in Daniel…helping to find a little peace of mind.

Envisioning sleep that I can't repeat, writing this down to understand.
To understand where I've just been; hidden within… deprivations play
pen; casting slowly downward, the night is fading, to dusk then day.
Eyes wide open.

Awakening to deep breathes and sigh.

Back against headboard, with gestures of undenied thoughts of

Visions…

© 24-September-2009
Visions

Writing Words...

Defined on paperless paper, writing cannot stop here.
Words flowing outward spilling onto dry floor, hot inside soothing
outside keeping warm.
Words with utensils that fail me repeatedly.
Writing it down until this pen runs out of style.

Cannot describe this feeling.
Just like freedom, throttled to its highest amp.
Words flowing funny at times mending pieces of the pi.,
Writing through the mixture of style and grace,
Montrose, privy, rotating this float, meter is moving,
Faster than typed words written down.

Defined on paper through spoken form,
Forming riddles and rhymes, capsule on its way to a place where it will
stay.
Words flowing inward spilling inside out.
Framing the best and the worst parts.

Dropping like gum drops in mouth first,
Spitting out the juices before the flavor runs out.
Balled-up paper becomes weight in the wind,
Finding new friends seems to justify within.

Words...

Defined on paperless paper, writing cannot stop here.
Words flowing outward spilling over in a cup,
Hot inside soothing outside keeping warm.
Words with utensils that fail me over and over,
Writing it down until this pen here runs out of ink.

© 4/15/2009
December 29, 2009
Words

Hope Floats

Hope floats.
Like goin' down the coast on a boat,
Lounging at sea on strong tides, that rip wide.

Rough enough to open the currant that will brush up lies,
Still and yet fine just like the winds, never see it coming until the end.

Breezes felt cool and crisp.
It is, called, faith.

Floating on a whim, hoping, praying, and riding out fate feels slim,
Mate and met at birth, fixed for life,
Taken deep breathes to fight, stayin' alive.

Washing up on shore, cold and freezing.
Hope floats and faith stands,
Stand the test, does not rest does more not less,
No stress, no mess.

Feelin' like singing,
Knowing faith rides, on a sleeve of strength.
No falsity, just faith.

© 22-March-2010
Hope floats

More than Words

More than words can say, Delay.
Demonstrating perfection for words lost in the sea of forgetfulness, conjuring up mixture of emotions, roaming about waiting for a chance to be used.

It's more than what a thought could ever be.
Even when the thought is aloud.
It is more than the gift received when it becomes the surprise offered so proudly.

It is more than the compassion felt for when the thought originally formed.
Planted on a mind so far and far.
It's more than the smile given not to mention a frown.

But,

More than words, that can't cry or scream words that could hurt or words that cure aloud.
It is more than that,
It is more than the Love ever received at heart.

Given from the start.
It is more than words could ever say.

REASONS

Reason to hope for things not seen.

Reason to learn for knowledge to gain.

Reason to Love for things hoped for.

The reason to live is for the precious gifts Life holds.

Hebrew 11:1

©11/28/1988
Reasons

Spoken

Delicate.
Un-canning, split into words that carry,
A mountain of majestic, super, intensified dialect tunes,
In tenor, interpretation of divers' tongue,
Powerful language.

Spoken Word

To intense to make sense for a culture and time.
That translates minds into thinking, thinking things in,
Rare form to perform weathered through storms, true nature.

Reproof from subtlety, sanctification in serene quiet movements of
Tai chi, purest form of movement on this side of the earth.
Moving, dancing, skipping beats to rhythmic chimes at the drop of a
dime,
Makes you talk, while stirring poetic pieces of Van Gogh colors
Refined.

An artist masterpiece of abstract design from the best minds,
Placed at feet, dropped in ears, heads do bob, sway to the seismic
metronome,
Given reflection and relaxation to escape fashion frame of mind, kind
to unwind,
The tone.

Eruption of heart not to corrupt from the start, into three sharp sparks.
Manifesting into shapeless circles, rings, rounded by,
Dictations of song spoken eloquently, spoken like crashing waves,
Moving up and down to cast renga tones into mantras unknown and to,
to the rest that, just can't feel this yet,

It's spoken word.

Word to the wise, filtering to the demised for the rest of,
Our lives, spoken to the keen, sharp, smart choices for the intellect, to
some,
Seen as strange and diverse in its on way to transform a genre to,
The art form that, lets you hear without saying a word.

Words on paper written down from the state of birth,
Bursting out into shades of color and meaning,
Spoken often, quenching spirit than soul,
Spoken word.
Formed life to be and to be again powerful as it is,
It was,
Spoken.

© 1-September-2009
Spoken Word

This Pen…

Mightier is this sword not me.

Who stands alone to fight this beast.

I turned my back to see.

But,

Looked too late to see you flee.

This book in hand, to look in a stance.

Could this reveal in ways how one may prance?

No words, no letters just the book I bare,

Standing with power as I fare.

I know it is real, everything I can feel.

But,

To look and search to find this pen,

I write the words to solve within.

©7/05/1989
This pen

Words

Wondered if this would be the last time, I'd speak without Saying words at all.
Found out different. I can do that roaming through halls that are decorative in lively streams of passion, I wondered what that looked like, found that passion and thought it was lost.

Kinder words said when the heart is soft instead.
Landing on a riverbed of streams that merge into lakes, lakes into dreams.
Drifting to sleep of good and sweet, eyes are heavy. Watering down tiredness, brown eyes wide and now shutting tight.

A little gentler staring and gazing into deep, shadowing and mimicking the dance, I do when I want to go to sleep. I can see the bed right down the hall, will not waste any more time trying to unwind you.

So,

I am going to turn in and call it, done.
You had plenty of time and you silenced your voice and shattered my ears from your fears, I'm traveling now, to the rear.

So,

No more words tonight,

Goodnight.

©1-March-2010
Last words

Enough Cry

Is it not enough to cry and then ask why.
Why do tears fill these eyes?
Fill with sorrow for those that suffer and hunger for food.
The world as known to mankind isn't kind and isn't sweet.

Is it not enough to cry for the faint at heart?
Steering matters from the start,
Daring to live another day,
Survival of the fit.

Is it not enough to cry for the child on TV, and see?
The enlarged tummy and the dry mouth with a nose runny, the flies
swarming around their little eyes and ears to not hear the buzz.

Is it not enough to cry and feel?
The pain, the hurt, the broken, the dying,
Is it not enough?

Raindrops are forming and clouds fill the air.
Next, let's catch a few out of despair.
Place several in my hand as they land,
Cup my hand like a sock, fills a glass of all the rain drops.

If I get the glass filled – I'll pray a prayer,
Climb the highest mountain and pour out the glass today of blessings
that will fill the land.

©November 4, 2009
Enough Cry

Repent I

I used to think of you.
How you graced the room when you entered through and even when
you left.
How you were poised.
I used to care so much for you,
And then you lost me boo.
Got my head spinning about the things you do.

Tried understanding, tried lollygagging about this and that.
Focused on your mouth, the way it formed to an almost perfect lie and
the pieces start to unravel to my eye.
Quickly, fast and in a hurry, skipping beats, rhyming feet,
Shame on me and shame on you for doing what we do.
I asked for forgiveness,
Did you?

Meek am I, humbled by, mistakes I take exclusive trips to kneel,
Asking, God to rinse me, to forever stay glad.
Forgiveness, I cry with solemn tears,
No madness, no sadness.

I cherish that I have rendered my fears, my worries, my stresses left it,
Where it should stay, now I do pray that you can do the same.
In some kind of way,
Repent I do.
Past and present and all unknown to view,
Let's get it right and clean it up to make it tight.

I can only ask that you do.

Simply put.

Repent.

Acts 3:19

© 7-March-2010
Repent I

Thoughts

Quick to resemble what you least forget,
Or not ... to tremble at the intense neglect,
For words spoken is distinct,
Passion to fervent waters
Do drink.

Quest to fire and fiery with might,
Moments of wander yet a mere gander,
Thoughts of every imaginable fruit,
Convey personable gesture of defeat,
Indulging minds with swift feet.

Calmer and yammer thoughts on paper.
Forming beautifully in moods of purple and grays.
Strokes of painted brushes streak across
The blank paper with,

Thoughts

Thoughts, collapsing into bill folds,
Crumbling under pressure for fresh and new.
Rising above the very thing that makes them,
Go off spells trouble for double in sweet softly spoken.

Thoughts of good and not bad,
Not complacent just sad.
Quick to resemble what you least forget,
Or not... to tremble at the intense neglect.
Words spoken too distinct.
Passion to fervent waters
Please do not drink.

© September 16, 2009
Thoughts

BACK AWAY

Back away from the desert storm that brews in the norm.
Cooling to low temperatures at night,
Covering face with hands of cloth,
Warming these arms to frigid air.
Shame the righteous of man.

Back away, back away, back away

Back away from the troubles of the world,
And what the world does bring.
Its calamity and timidity rampages through the cities at night.
The terror heightens at levels that decibels do ring loudly,
Hearing over the cries of a world for healing feeling.

Back away

Back away from the turbulence of falling hearts that run,
Stammer in complexity and full of jealousy,
Deceit shows her colors in dark purples and black, signs of the times,
Cannot be declined from the ears of scorners, persecutors, and forgers.
Back away.

Back away from the naysayers that drown in their own hatred,
Shadowed and vexed by their past trouble finds its way to their hearts,
Slowly watch where feet do stand and run, quickly toward the sun.
Mark your forehead with pure oil, kneel and pray for Christ returns,
Return to a child that have turned from their wicked ways,
Come quickly oh God!
Please show us the way.

Let's prepare the way, prepare as Christ coming is nearby.

Crossroads

I don't know if the words I put down will rhyme.

I don't know if the words I jot down will matter in this poem of mine.

But can you try this on for size.

Dishonesty makes things invalid.

And

Lies make things complex.

Trouble causes denial.

But love conquers all to whoever felt defeat.

**©11/21/1989
Crossroads**

In The Crowd

When you wanted to hide

They saw you.

When you cried, they laughed.

But,

When they left, you stood still,

You were the one, in the Crowd.

When you did not want to be there,

You had no choice.

When you ran, they knew who you were.

Because

You stood out, in the Crowd.

Wherever you are

You will be there,

Somewhere, in the Crowd.

1Timothy 4:12-16

©4/29/1999
In the Crowd

No Fault Line

Willing to involve, matters which engage sympathies of the heart,

Terms of endearment and torn apart,

Inside-out, outside-in.

Willing to impart, an imaginable life, a fresh breath, a start.

Offloading luggage before you part.

Packing old memories from a loaded past to outlast

Is this going too fast?

Can you throw away time?

Ball it up without looking back to un-whined.

Reruns of a faded life

Re-whined.

Understand, things take slow turns.

Driving toward no fault lines.

No fault lines here, there, or anywhere.

© July 27, 2009
No fault lines

Procrastination

Misfortune for the one who doesn't take the opportunity to,

Use time to their advantage instead of making sitting a passion.

Misguided future of those who ramble and wait for a path not to take one,

That is far too long.

Wondering where did time go? By and bye.

So, keep sitting on the side lines, while wait,

Eventually

Procrastination will be a good running mate.

Colossians 3:1-2

© 5-25-1993
Procrastination

Quickness

Quicken to fit Quickness,

In grasping life once held, leading to lead not Fail.

Carrying time in a pocket full.

Quick to hurry to scattered and broken finds,

Following paths of wrong instruction, sigh.

And

Purpose to plan and plan to fail before starting.

Reason for living now changing, changing to change the mindset,

Set before a road well-traveled before.

Quickens for life in living now,

Now will not resolve the empty kind.

Content to quickly rush through a pattern will due.

A rushing wind now blows you, away a broken relay,

Not grounded from the start.

Life is more than that, so live and live, but not too fast.

©11/17/2009
Revised 12/23/2009
Quickness

Sand Trap

Sand at feet, catching some between the toes,
Feels like earth left its crust crumbled and cold.
Walking on cushion and grain to clean this soul to refrain.

Sand through these hands, gritty as a clam, rough and tough.
Sand at feet, warm and meek, wild, and free settled and complete.
Sand, oh sand bare and fare quite contraire.

Sand dunes in May watching the ocean play, roaring in octaves tray
notes called, tranquility. Listening to counterpoints sound off ...sand.
Sand in hair, waving in the air and the wind is my back blowing... and
bending me to change my course of action settle and remain calm while
losing to the grind moving quickly downward, slowly watching the sky
rise higher than I can see it.

Sand trapped by life and not letting go. Letting God manage all things
and everything.
Trust him, trust within trusting more than the last breath, I take in this
Sand Trap.

Matthew 6:31

©12-August-2010
Sand Trap

Twisted

Caught up in the caught up not ashamed.
Being sincere in lust and in love with the essence of
What came?

Trying something new for a change, from the view it looks like
temperature got you all,
In a frazzle, bedazzled.

Looking to what was hip something to do,
Something to have but, then again it shows in all the unstable
Ways you have.

Riding on the hope and a dream that it'd be different,
From what had failed inhibitions.

Playin' the game for a tiring cause in keeping alive a missed,
Opportunity to cash in on the odds… disturbingly enough an attempt,
Gone wrong in all the missed guided direction of ….

Twisted

Leaving behind what keeps you afloat for all the
Right reasons for not wanting to make quick decision,
Much too fast for the course taken for unfamiliar territory,
Not claimed.

Twisted, and all caught up in the game,
Wound up in love.
Dropped out cause' you wanted gone.
Trippin' still in fashion for you, wearing it well these days,
Are you?

Twisted

© December 22, 2009
Twisted

Age tingles

Skin sheds and new skin appears it is a wonder that things just don't disappear.
A new person is there I can see it somewhere, within this skin. It has been years,
Changing' and still evolving into this woman, woman.

It's a wonder, the time doesn't slow, pause, or wait while gravity takes its toll and,
Begins to escalate,
Slowly,
Taking its toll on a body that seemed invincible...so inevitable, incredible,
This woman, woman.

Moment by moment. Tick, tock on the clock moves,
And
Intent still spoons that there is still room in a,
More prevalent than an epiphany waiting,
This woman, woman.

Appear, vanish, and fade. New skin, a mole, a freckle just strayed,
Eyes see in the mirror reflecting relevance of
Truth that matters,
This woman, woman.
The second the hand strikes again on time.

What once was is no more, now left behind.
And changes occur to remind that with each shedding of skin a life is still, adorned and waiting to be embraced, faced, and paced.

Age tingles with a cringle,
Abiding the rules, following patterns of plans at hand,
A motivating factor enables to keep focused on the
Prize waiting until sunrise.
To glance with a stance and to know that,
Age is changing me.

©December 18, 2009
Age tingling

Harmony

Harmony is meeting balance here.
Meeting for the first time and not the last,
Face – to – face in rarest form.
Harmony stares correcting, evening things adorn.
Creating parallels of contrast in plain sight.
Or maybe horizontally, perpendicular dimensions into shaping human delight.

Harmony is standing there, watching to embrace the victory of balance in body, mind, and soul.

Harmony

Harmony is ringing for a song to sing,
A hymn to hum for a little while.
The song becomes passion inside,
Inside to bring out healing that waits by faith.

Harmony...
Ringing for a song to sing,
A hymn in Psalms, Proverbs sung.
Humming for a little while for the passion inside,
Inside to bring out the healing that waits by faith.

©October 21, 2009
Harmony

I BET

*I bet you think this poem is about you, you and it's just for you, to know.
I bet no one has ever told you, the human creature you are and that God
is letting you know that you are a wonder.*

*I bet no one has ever told you that you are a treasure, a charm and
many gifts are in you for telling the world your story.*

*I bet no one has ever told you the power you possess is in your hands
that will change lives to the people around you.*

*I bet no one has ever told you that you are royalty and that you have
been called blessed beyond measure.*

*I bet no one has ever told you that winter, summer, spring, and fall is
consumed in your freedom called, your season. You season to blossom
and bloom beyond your understanding.*

I bet...

*I bet no one has ever told you just how awesome you are or how
beautiful you are, how amazing that you can be from your smile to
laughter, even the gleam in your eye and the sparkle that can't be
denied.
I bet ...*

*I bet songbirds sing to the heavens to rejoice that God sees and blesses
them and God takes care of their needs just like you.
And
I bet you may feel unappreciated at times because you're rushing on a
dime to see everyone else is being treated kind.
And that your efforts go undefined in time, God sees, and God knows
just who you are.
I bet ...
I bet that blessings are on the way to you, coming to overtake you,
where there isn't room enough for you to hold it all.*

I bet...

And,

I know you are favored beyond what you know, God's plan for you is known.
God will give you strength to carry on, win your battles over the enemy and give you rest with peace and joy.
But I bet you are more loved than you'll ever know and you should celebrate for there are great things for you. This I know.

©2-June-2008
I bet

Possibilities

The Possibility

Meeting someone on a wonderful day like today becomes second to none.
But now a smile just a second away can cover the emptiness that was,
The possibility that something good is happening right now, makes for true beginnings.

The possibility of warm thoughts enter at the right time makes for positive energy,
The possibility that blessings are in the earth and believing that,
Makes for faith to take its course.
And
The possibility that encouragement waits for the opportunity to do so,
Says all things are possible.

So, make it that possibility of believing just that.

Matthew 19:26

©December 24, 2009
Possibility

Private Thoughts

Did you ever just wonder off in thought?
And
Thought you were the only one in the room, alone just a thought or
two,

Realizing that you were confined by ultimate deep travel in space and
time for a mere nanosecond of everything that happened or is
happening right now, consumed,
Yet not doomed.

The fact that you're not speaking aloud should tell you something,
Something like you, are keeping it to yourself, that personality trait
the Kinsey topology, isn't it funny, I'm not alone in the class of the
non-theoretical.

Private thoughts,
Creating collectively gathered captured images of digital graphs into
play, like iPod gone mad for a thousand more songs on a 1 terabyte of
memory, right!

Private thoughts,
Belong to a still frame after frame resuming wonderfully, pleasurable
factors of nice elevator music, going up?

Private thoughts,
Of moonlight and moon dust raining down to touch a bit at a time,
place a little in the pocket for a dime, ground level please.

Thought about whatever you wanted to, with no one to ask,
And
Then ask,
What are you thinking about? A magnificent sigh, a ponder, a gesture,
comes over you to realize the words come out faster than you can,
Say, nothing.
Laughter takes over inside to realize.

Private thoughts that belong to no one else but you, created and mastered by you for you it is all yours!

Another deeper breath, than before, knowing deep inside that you're doing it again, why? Because it's your private thoughts and you don't have to tell a soul.

July 20, 2009©
Private thoughts

Something Real

*In the essence of time, I can hear your heartbeat and I am listening to
Love.*
*I am listening to tear drops, I'm watching hands softly wipe away the
rain.*
*I'm looking at laughter and smiles appear my way, looks like a rainbow
at the end of
Day.*
*I see fragments left behind on a back trail of memories, I see
reminiscing,*
Through a heart that is fluttered with conversation, it's good. yes!
It is a good thang,'
*Waiting for the feeling to burst right out of my chest, splattering gold
like sprinkles called, Love dust.*

I'm feeling the warmth embrace of soft cellos play,
I'm feeling sincere,
Rushing back to child like thoughts that race in and out,
Characterizing what it feels like to know, knowing what to know.

Knowing what to say, in the essence of time.
I can hear the bump, bump, bump, fade faintly,
Lowering the echo in my head.

Hearing the words, the sound, a voice,
Utter the smallest and most powerful words "Love."
Loving the way that sounds.

©December 18, 2009
Something Real

Who will Love Her?

Who will love her for her full lips that would pay to kiss?
Who will love her hips that are wide and curved?
Who will love her thighs that embrace thunder?
Who will love her?

Who will love her Blackness if he won't?
And
Who will love her dark brown eyes that feature stars that twinkle in her
smile and glisten in the night?
Who will love her song that she sings playin' alone?
Who?

Who will love her charisma and the sway in her walk?
Queen in stride, scepter in one hand across her bosom.
Where are the men that loved her, wanted to be at her side, bear
children.
Call them rely, rely on, trust in God that granted her earth, showing the
true nature of her.

Who?

Who will love her once again?
Show her she is still in, a goal and the apple in his eye.
Calling her his sweet princess, filling her basket with un-measurable
pride.
Who will sit with her, hold her hand, lead her to her throne, follow her
and call her jasmine and gold.

Who?

Who will go to aid her, support her backside when weakness falls,
clothe her from the cold, watch over her, stand by her side, show her
this is why.
Who will give her comfort for her pain in the night, lay with her at the
Nile?

Who?

Who is willing to stay and not go, show her his arms are still
Open wide.

©7-March-2010
Who will love her?

Lovely

Lovely as the day is long and bearing the weight of the day, sighing in relief, pausing in belief.

Lovely is the afternoon thinking I will stay.

I am inhaling sunshine and exhaling moonlight, it feels right.

*Lovely is the deep breathes taken for the challenge is difficult but, I am
Embracing joy, indulging happiness.
Lovely is not dull.
I'm caressing love, brushing off the hate in time that will fade away.*

Lovely this way

*Is the wire sparked to charge my heart, filled with energy for a quick spark of,
Wonderful, sweet, and nice, lovely is what is.
The spirit to my life keepin' it all just lovely.*

©17-May-2010
Lovely

World's Finest

It is smooth and soothing.
It is rich and inexpensive.
It is satisfying without denying.

It is most pleasing all over the world,
In three shades and textures.
Once you crave, there is desire for more than one at time, or more
than what can be handled.

The World's finest that one dollar can buy.
It's sometimes easy to melt if sitting too long.
Easy to freeze when waiting and waiting for the first bite.
Called the World's Finest and it has different names.
But please do not tell?

World Finest

© 8/04/1993
World's Finest

Writing music

I am writing music.
Like rain drops falling, like drops, onto face, glistening like night stars
upon moonlight rays.

I am writing music.
Like I want to play all notes are silent and quiet until the sound fades,
Placed on paper thin sheet-notes that fall in line on raw silk paper,
Flowin' in beautiful octaves of C.

Ah…

I am writing music.
Like the jazz style you hear playin' on sax, piano and drums, acoustics
like music of Miles Davis, Earl Klugh like… Joe Sample, John Coltrane
style music like, grown up type music, sounds of Tito Puente and Valente
type music.
Cruising with convertible back down on sunset while the sun is set.

I am writing music.
Like the sounds of smooth secular hits, hearing acapella pitch type
music, just let it play, let it play all night and dance.
Last on the floor til' the last note still stands.

Writing music.
Something you want to hear, real music in your ear so very near and
dear music, that captures your thoughts, taking you back, back type
music.

I am writing music.
To make you un-whined, still holdin' on to time while praise is on the
mind,
Using that last dime for the music box to play just one more chime.

I am writing music.
Like rain drops falling, like drops onto face, glistening like the stars
upon moonlight cast down in rays of music notes in C minor.

©2/13/09
Writing music

A Talk with God

God still speaks in the midnight hour.

Dipping into man's spirit,

Awakening into the night into the dawn of morning,

Into day God's still listening quietly, patient.

Peaceful touch of the heart and

Beats as the only sound of the night.

God still speaks when listening to the heart and spirit of calm.

A still voice inside called ministry at its best.

A talk with God overcomes all understanding.

God is speaking.

©March 3, 2009
A Talk with God

Calling

In the darkness of the day, the light of you shines my way, bringing unspeakable peace.
The uncertainty of not knowing what the world will transpire.

In you, there is the confidence of hope in a desperate and cruel place.
The strength of you feeds my spirit and the power in your words heals marrow to bone.

Supplement of a daily walk is a vitamin not missed,
I care to have you around friend.
The charisma of life brought through ministering songs revives praise in me.

Over and over, I am young again, the child renewed in mind which was once confused but now no more.
A yesterday's daydream is a tomorrow's vision.

I look to you for the foundation of the future that spills over into my quest of fulfilling a calling long before I knew.

I wish to have you here, very near and close all the time, a new creature created in your image and a temple to house your spirit confirmed in me.

Sprinkle the garments of fine linens with a new declaration of freedom a due.
A new song to shake the walls of a world so misdirected by a guiding force of disbelief.
But in this restoration will come and the captives will be freed.

©11/4/1997
Call

I   N   S   P   I   R   E

Lord, you the writer better than I.
You are the song of psalms, the apple of my eye.

You are the inspiration of life given me.
Unfolding the passions and secrets, which prosper me.

Words of expression clutter in me.
Yet you touch me, and words are clear, without fear always knowing
that you're near.

I hear and tears run faster than I cry.
Lord, you are better than I.

Flexing in strength more than the wise,
Bolder than I know to be.

Yes Lord, it is me.

Yes, you inspire me.

© 3/31/2008
Revised
December 21, 2009

Someone to Bless

Looking for someone to bless today.
Searchin' all day and all the way.
Looking for that right face,
Searching almost gone astray.

Knowing in the spirit there is someone,
Who needs today, has a want today. Said, a prayer today.
Blessed by someone, anyone today.

So, looking and looking even going out my way.
To see if, I see what I can see today.
Looking for that someone to bless,
In all nations, in every continent, in every forgotten place.
There is someone to bless, and to give today.

Is anyone there?
Because I am looking for someone to feed, to clothe, and to give to today.
Looking for that right face,
Searching almost gone astray.

Show me Lord and I will go.
Go out of my way to bless someone.
Does not matter if it's far and away.
Does not matter if it's just someone, I can find today.

© 15-June-2010
Someone to Bless

Stage

As, I stand here. I see you lookin' at me, wondering what Am I doin'
here, standing there, given you somethin' that, you might want to hear,
worth hearin' deep in your inner ear.

Yet, I'm crossing into your territories, being renewed in mind,
creating a pulse runnin' through veins, simple complexity for your
extremities, feeling alive.
Watching me as, I form my lips to every word that spills like water,
catching a few in your lap, picking it up to propagate these verbs into
a language.
Marinate on it.
You are hearing it, hearing spirit, soul in body.

On stage, the words come out better than rehearsed, clearer than
memorized lines, educated over time. But I am led. Led by spirit,
touched by God, so I'll take his hand, as I'm giving out parts of me
and all of him, by his word and through his word.

Feelin' fixtures of today, yesterday, and forever. That's his word that
never dies, never takes sides, can't lie, or be denied, still being proven
over time. Let's just un-whined and watch, watch how the truth will
be misinterpreted, cut and dry, reaching out to the audience and seeing
these readers.
Wondering how can this be defined from a new art form called,
reprised?

The podium is my world stage teaching and preaching with
conviction, handing down doctrine, putting you in a different frame of
mind, sharing the biblical canon, showing the apocrypha in slow, hand
motions, expressions of evangelical courses called, outreach.

It's relentless in stride no pride, hangin' on tides of goodness,
freshness, necessary to do this, complete this book of my journey,
turning, leaning toward creating and finishing what's started, never
parted from who I am, here on this stage.

© 8.12.2010
Stage

The Way U Love Me

I love the way you love me; I do.
I love the way you touch my soul and give to me, the way you do.
I love the way you love me, on grains of my wrongs and my right,
Holy Spirit Do I.

I love the way you love me and the way you make me give, the way.
The way I give and say, I want to do your service.
Heaven waits for humbled doers and givers, Holy Spirit pour out, pour
out today.

I love the way you love me and the way you are my friend, teaching me
and showing me,
How Christ is in me. Sampling me, assessing me, keeping me.
I love the way you love me; I do.

I love the way you touch my soul; I do.
I love you and even on grains of all the mistakes,
Holy Spirit Do I.
Long to get it right.

© 6/1/2008
The way u love me

The Word says I Can

You can do all and anything, it is whatever you say.
The power of your words will change every circumstance today.
You can do all and everything whatever is believed it shall be.

That is God's word today.

In the mist of the storm know that God is and everything he is to you and more.
He can be the blessing to change your life within and whatever believed it shall be.

God is the same today, yesterday, and forever more.
He can, He will, He is the source.
God is.
He can, He will, He is everything,
For greater is he that is within you,
U can do all things through Christ that strengthens you.

And

Would you believe less than who u really are in Christ?
You have the mind of Christ.
Stronger in might, stronger in one accord.
Be it to what u set Ur mind to do.
Yell!

Come forth, come forth.
So shall it be unto you.

© 17-June-2010
The Word says I can

Where is my friend?

I've searched the oceans, I searched the sky, and I searched the sands and could not find.
Where is my friend Lord and where have they gone?
And yet, I think about all the lives that have been lost.

I think about the ones that, I touched along the way and the journey for today, though not perfect nor can I say. Yet, I think about the ones that were missed because of self pride, and I think about the hurt and demise and still I wonder.

Where is my friend Lord? I don't want them left behind, I stammer, I cry, fall on my knees, repent do I. I preach, I teach and hearken with a voice so loud, and I know Heaven hears, I can't be proud, where is my friend Lord?

I believe the word will find them and something I've said is rooted deep inside them, still wondering and I still cry save my friend, not one or two, save the many, don't want to see them perish or die.
Send the word Lord.
Send the word Lord, because cannot leave not one waiting, or one left behind.

Romans 3:23

©6-July-2010
Where is my friend

WISDOM

I can't decide for you when you've already thought it through. I will give,
You a reasonable smile and grin and wait on your reply.
I can't give you all the answers when most you already know.

The answers to ones you have common sense to, I'll give you a chance
to plunder over all the thoughts to.
I can point in the direction I think you should go.

Wisdom

I have traveled down that same path, I know it's safe and peaceful,
smooth and balanced, wise and pleasant, warm and joyous.

Wisdom

If you choose to take another route other than one destined for your
life, then,
I'll send you a prayer and angels while you're on your way,
For know that wisdom will come when you ask her to show her face. It
won't deny you an antidote, she will rely on what makes her; she is
determined by her poise and elegance.
So, rely on her to show you the way.

Just know that the path is traveled by many along the way.

Proverbs 9:10

© 3-May-2010
Wisdom

Gifted Hands

These hands of thee sweet with charity.
Forgiving with all honesty, before Thee, thy gifted hands are these.
Thank thee with full heart.
Standing before thee dropping tears on thy alter.
Blessing me, thy gift these hands to me, I do cherish thee.

Thankful to thee for this humility, to the heavenly.
Thee I sing oh! Lord you are God of all Creation and of my soul.
Life you give to thee, where grace abounds for me.
I kneel to honor thee.
Blessing me, thy presence allows for Love to explore.

Oh God.

How do I deserve thy mercies upon these hands that do miracles I cannot even see?
Casting immeasurable colored pictures called dreams into my mind of vivid, inter-twines of healing.
Choosing me before I chose myself and dropping portions of your spirit upon me how do I offer a seed to thee with thanksgiving?

These hands gifted to thee I do thank,
With them I honor thee… I bow down before you Oh God!
The God of Abraham, Isaac and Jacob do I prepare thee my offering.
So, tithes I do bring and with this seed I store on reserve the blessings of the Lord that you may continuously touch me and that, which is yours.

Exalted high in the heavens, here oh God.
I prepare the offering and to thee I bring.
The best of me.
Daughter, sister, aunt, cousin, and friend.

Thankful to thee for this humility to the heavenly.
Thee I sing oh! Lord you are God of all Creation and my soul.
Life you give to thee, where grace abounds for me.
I kneel to honor thee.
Blessing me, thy gift these hands to me, I do cherish thee.

© 24-May-2010
Revised 21-June-2010
Gifted Hands

Good Respect

*With all due respect. Remember first is last, last is first when it's your
turn in line.*
Never forgetting to respect and maintain composer in kind.
Grab hold of success and keep in mind, who and where you are
At all times.

Never slipping is a rare find. Invest good, in good times.
Fun time in carrying a good attitude all the while.

And

Good respect for self would be just fine.

©12/19/90
 Revised
Good Respect

No Vanity

I was selfish.
I was zealous and proud.
Smashing down pride with a smile.
Heard that I ran out of style,
I am conformed to endless boundaries, borders, and bridges,
Crossing over to create a better path.

I was a thief, stole hearts.
Managed to steer emotions to harden face to stone cold.
I am inspired by soft touches, arms wrapped, strapped by sweetness.

I have not mastered indulgence for the sake of philandering bragging
rights; gaining a new friend tonight or Enemies will unite.
Quiet the mind to thinking and suggesting irony.

I am folding pages of memories, collecting sketches for my future.
And
Leavin' legacy for being a childless mother to my nephews the children
I will love.

I have reasoned in mind, setting up the hopes, valuing an array in line,
in scope, focused on a larger view of the world, world, not trying to be
Giovanni or Baldwin of today, staying away.
I'm just bein' me so that the name will be in a framed, or fame.
I was lookin' for something else but, I'll accept this just the same.
Just want to receive the blessin' o' what I owe my God because.
He knows.

© 7-March-2010
No Vanity

The Champh

In case in your mind, you wondered why, then you know that curiosity,

Travels aside.

In case you thought,
You were wrong, you happen to be right.

And for strange reason, you have fallen asleep so, wake up and realize,

There is no defeat!

Today is a new day! Come on champ be the champ you sought out to be.

Keep on going you can do all things, just believe.

Philippians 4:13

©10/8/1985
Champ

This Man

A Black-American is he, this man, a man to be, he can.

Tracing through roots in time; establishment of his kind.
This man is he which is to define.

A man first is he, being all, he can be.
Finding identity, this man.
Finding what is right and just,

King of kin.
King of Royalty, there is loyalty and nobility.

Finding tranquility.

King, he is indeed,

Freedom in his hand.

This man, this man

African American is he. Black American to be.

©1/24/09
This man

Well Done

I caught a Glimpse of you in a dream.
I thought it was yesterday.
It was somewhere in a closed room of colored walls and a white pearl
floor,
Music played from a harp and a sound that placed you at the door.

The harp created sounds of strings with one solid stroke, I stood there
watching from the corner of the room and you entered, with a smile, a
smile so sweet. You asked for a dance and to take your hand, your words
I still hear, and the music played, and we danced.

Angels shared in the joy of dance and pranced, skipped and more
musical instruments filled this room. You suddenly stopped! The music
stopped!
You Lord.

In the middle of the floor, a tear dropped from your eye and these words
spoken out of your mouth yet longing to be heard.

I was just a witness but not surprised.

It may have seemed, the clouds above were blocking the sunlight from
reaching the beauty of your face and you reached your outstretch arms
toward heaven, and the clouds moved. Yet, sunlight rays filled this
place.

Your words so clear like spring water from a mountain said, "So Let
My Will Be Done."
And let the people say, well done!
Amen.

©12/15/1997
Well done

Quote

"In everything you do
Let Faith rain in life.
Remember no one can lead you,
Astray
No one can take away,
for
The life God has purposed for your destiny".

Isaiah 43:1-4

©11/28/1988
A Quote

The Content of My Character

*The trouble lies ahead if the content of my character is to be at stake.
It is not me to be found guilty of my skin tone or the shade and color of
my eyes.*

So, who is it?

*That may plague me with their incantations and their arrogant minds,
I may wish to say it is not the content of my character to be at stake but,
it must, be my presence that stalks in the midnight hours.*

*The content of my character is clear and quiet in the wind and its words
distinctly heard a loud with a realness of vibration and a willingness to
strive.*

The content of my character and my skin is not to be denied.

*My skin is not the one held in a secluded hell hole but, it's the mind of
that character held to bondage.*

*My character is proud and free.
My character is me.*

And

With me there is might, strength, and bravery to stand strong.

The content of my character is peculiar and most of all unique.

©2/1/1990
Content of my character

Climate Change

By circumstance we the people are fixed by environmental climates that enhance our depth thinking illogically while repercussions stand and waits on denial of what's not known.

By no fault of our own, a one but, no one owns up to the mistake of ignorance; it's too much like right than wrong.

Rising temperatures give way to global warming changes translating trouble may be a warning ahead, trouble ahead, fixed by being convinced – we the people buy more green to change our minds into being justified, satisfied into saying, "I think I'll buy that hybrid or EV".

Wait a second. This has got to be social engineering of society's fixation on green.

Warmer is hotter, hotter becomes hottest.
Cold is colder, becoming coldest yet,
Rain and humid mixture causing distress,
Creating for uncomfortableness and hysteria for dooms day ahead.

Truth is God is still God.
God does not need help in decision making.
Since the earth is in fullness thereof ... then it's clear enough to know, the universe in all its magnificence is a wonder that needs no explanation from God.

It is just what it is! Climate change. Is In his hands.

© 23-September-2009
Climate changes

You are ...

Why should you be surprised?
Designed and hand crafted through a specified eye, the perfection of God's hand.
You are Woman. Woman you are the kaleidoscope of DNA ancestry, a tapestry to bring you to this point in your life and yet, you may ask who AM I?

The story is told that you derived from the woman they called Eve, first of her kind on the earth. Manifested from chemistry in God's laboratory and inspected by the angels of the most high angelic host. The purification of your composition was determined by God for God and with the witnesses of two and the entire heaven to say "Yes" she is a split image of the side of God that reflects her.

Wisdom, purification, delicate, moral, value, man's mate, soul partner, child bearer to indoctrinate, a balancer, a dancer, a watchtower, a director, a star. And she Ask Who AM I? Do you not know your initial of 'S' is the same in Jesus' name… meaning spirit. You made in the likeness not the unlikeness, perfected after the words filled in Adam's mouth, woman you are 'bone of my bone' and 'flesh of my flesh' and yet She ask Who Am I?

She is You. Cast out and cast in time and time again. The filler behind the comma and the period when it ends. It started with you and finished by you, the caress of soft hands that prepare the hot meal, supports, holds, resolves, manages, and balances the cry her children. Tears of laughter, sadness and hurt, confusion and disparity and yet She Ask Who AM I?

I tell you no story and tell you no lies. But you are the pillar and salt of the earth defined. God said, he can do it again. You are the first but, you won't be the last. You are she and she is you. By God and for God that is not denied. He loves you and the first to love you and never does he turn from you, deny you or lie to you. He is God. He created you in his image to be admired, respected, and adored by man. You are an antidote of the missing language that your words speak and again don't ask who you are. Because God had already given you a name before you were born.

Rise up and call yourself blessed. Blessed by nations.
Rise up and call yourself Daughter, Daughter of the earth foreseen by heaven.
Rise up and call yourself Woman that doesn't reflect self pity, doubt, self-hate or regret.
You are Woman and Woman is what you're called to be!

©January 3, 2007
You Are

Self-Check

Check.
Check 1. Check 2.

The mic won't bend unless I bend it to, to the sound effects that's all around you,
Bouncing off walls into the halls, vibrating through seams and cracks,
Getting' through to you.
I'm checkin' self against self and not against you,
Can only do it for me and not for you.

Check. Check. It's my sound effect,
Tryin' to collect my attitude, rearrange what I found, collecting on frowns.
Past and present issues changing, rearranging, the cause of this or that.
Creating a new revenue that's in review with the IRS tax adrenaline.

Balancing out the levels of frustration of becoming null and void, acting like androids.
Watch out could be a surrogate clone, switching stations like I'm changin' friends, cashing in on all dividends.
Checking me against myself reviewing in the mirror
Repeatedly, I say.

Watching what I'm sayin' and when I'm saying it.

So, check 1, Check 2.

The mic won't bend unless I bend it to...to the sound effects that's all around.
Bouncing off walls into the halls, vibrating through seams and cracks, I'm,

Getting through to you.
I'm checking self against self and not against you.
I'm the only one that can do for getting this together forever.
And ever revolving into view.

©July 2, 2009
Self check

UNDERSTAND....

*There is so much to learn about who you are everyday that makes me
want to cry.*
*There is so much to enjoy about you, that it makes me want to have you
here all the time.*

A person like you should understand,
What gifts you possess that others seem to cling to.
You are so rare and precious that,
One cannot help to understand why.

Why others like to be around you,
Like a song once sang you are priceless.

Understand.

© 07-24-2003
Understand

A Bridge

If a bridge is built to get to the other side,
I would build it for you to cross.
I would build Tavern-Tine tile with initials made in gold.
I would place red carpet at your feet for royalty.
I would prepare a guide for things you don't know.
And
Place at your hands a book called wisdom, on the other side of the
bridge.
I would place a podium with a book resting upon it, that would store all
that a man can be. Storing God's secrets for a character so meek.

The book would read.
You are a boy today, so play.
A son so train.
A brother that learns to protect.
An uncle so show honor.
A leader so build integrity.
A mentor that leads.
A teacher that instructs in truth.

All these things and more, that will someday make you a father, a man
and respected, so that you can provide, protect, and have purpose.
A vision for the family to shelter from the storms,
But
Learn from your mother and do as your told.
Find how she exudes in Faith and Love to rear her only Son.

©November 17, 2009
Bridge

Because

Because you know that Love always has a home here.
Here in me and here with me.

Because you know that Love always will be alive here,
Here with me.

Because you know that Love always has a place here,
Here with me.

Let Love be, let love be, giving time to grow, heal and rekindling each
day and each day, Love has a way of letting us know that it reins.

© *August 10, 2009*
Because

Brother

Brother can you see that purpose is destined for you,
In view, in the path of righteousness for intended happiness.
Brother can you see that love abounds much for you, in reach, in reach
of you freely given unconditionally, attainably, and phenomenally.

Brother listens.

Brother can you see that dreams are within your grasp, held by clasp
of strength,
Staring you in preview and on the road for divine intervention,
invention with no prevention that would cause' you no tension.
Brother can you see that hopes are high and that we're on your side, to
see you stride with pride.

Brother hears.

Brother can you see that victory is at the finish line for you,
It's on course for you, in scope of plans with open hands, destiny and
where apathy is beneath you.
Finish the race, finish the race son, step up, there is much to be done.
Step up, there is respect in what you do, step up and take your position,
just get through! No time for non-existence, your pre-existence tells its
story in Genesis chapter 1.

Brother sees.

In retrospect God's plans are higher than your plans, God's thoughts
are higher than your thoughts, God's ways are mild and meek, modest,
just to start.
Brother relinquish the battle with thin your heart, stirs and pulls at your
mind, tryin' to unwind the trouble confined, yes just one lace at a time.
Trying to mend a solution that you will not find.

Given time to mediocrity in your face with much velocity, to deny.
I love you to tell you no lies to tell you, you're my brother.

© *21-June-2010*
Brother
 "Happy Father's Day"

Grandmother

Knowing where you are relaxes my spirit to be still.
I was once restless knowing of your discomfort and that you needed
your release to come quick.

I begin to reminiscence of young childhood thoughts of me, that little
girl sitting on your high-back living-room couch.
I sat patiently, in that big roomy house, old and tattered looking, but it
was yours's grandmother.

I remember that little girl sitting as she was being watched from above,
the pink living-room wall of pictures, those three men looking down at
me, their eyes seemed to follow you from anywhere in that room, even
if you moved or even asleep those men. I called them the three forgotten
Kings, so dark, dim, weary and scoping with a real concern.

Yes, I remember well grandmother.

You would sing from the old brown attached service porch, washing
yesterday's clothes, and hanging out the damp ones to dry on the
clothesline in the backyard.
Your cupboards were full of all your favorite can goods.

I remember well.

The shopping cart you pushed from the grocery store miles away. You
were strong with a willingness and all your better days are behind you
now. Contentment came early for you grandmother.

The hymns of old Baptist church songs sung from your lips, as you were
around the house. And now, everything is clear to me, I see the Lord
has gazed upon you and borrowed time has elapsed.

"To be absent from the body is to be present with the Lord."

Yet, I hear the Lord Say, "I will come in a twinkling and pain will be no more."

So, he came and now I know you are home and safe, away from this place on earth and now, I can rejoice.

©*10/30/1990*
Grandmother

Hand to Mouth

Fixed on the words spoken heard with warm ears.
Hearing repeatedly playing in the background like a scene from a movie,
Covered with perplexed thoughts and reason for calm and slowly, touched by a subtle comfort, southern like, gentle like.

Rough edges now curved in an enthusiastic measure of patience.
Covered by a soft hand, caring touch with love like as she kneels to pull the blanket over; just like the bear over her cubs, she protects. She guides and watches.

A cough sounds in another room as she smiles and says, I will be right back.
She enters another room filled with the smell of cough syrup, Vicks, and a blowing humidifier. She places one hand to mouth and with her free hand grabs a hand towel on the nightstand to pat down a misty face and moist neck.
She looks with concern and love; compassion fills her to give freely.

And

All night and between rooms watching over her little ones, she places hand to mouth with hands of healing until the last cough has stopped.

She is a mother doing what's best and doing what's right. Why would it be any different?

©December 17, 2009
Hand to mouth

JAZZ MAN...

I used to watch from the seat of the couch, while he sat in the living room, in a chair pulled up next to the stereo.

The old 33's piled up on the floor in a sequential order for the next artist to play, mic in hand, ready to announce the next, "player up".

The base on the speakers bumpin' hard against the walls, I think the neighbors can hear, cause' it's pounding down the hall.
Yes, it's pounding; hard but, it's what made him feel good at the end of the day as sounds of fading train horns go passing bye... bye... bye.
He smiles and laughs like it was the best taste of scotch on his lips, he ever had; it was Jazz "he'd go".

"Hear that sound going blimp, bop, bop, da bee, da bop, razz, tazze! Yea, that's it blows your horn! Blow your horn! Now! Now that's music, ha! You cannot get no better than that, ha, ha, let's go to work, that's the jazz players, quiet, listen, listen to the instruments, if you listen a little closer, you can hear the man blow his breathe down the pipe of the horn.

Yes, that's it! Do you hear it?

Man, "he'd go", "I use to dance and dance to that sound of that jazz. And jazz is my middle name, and my last name is salsa, Maranga. Tito Puente, Hector Lavoe and Cecilia Cruz kept me cha-cha' all night long.

I am dancing and dancing all night long. I'll be dancing next time you see me again.
But just call me Jazz Man.

©12/19/07
Jazz Man
'Dedicated To: Clarence B. Scott Jr.'

Uncle

*I captured you in a smile; a warm hug and a pleasant how are you?
down to your poised stature of character is he.
The ad vet Tennis player and artist, the artist and craftsmen, the singer
and songwriter all in me.
The Blood line, our Lineage, this Lifeline inside inspires me to cope
...glorious hopes,
Encouraged me to be when you never knew you did inquire of me.*

You...

*Uncle, father, brother, my mother's blood in you and me, both sharing
in commonality, whole heartedly.*

*I often aspire to find a man that carries himself in your likeness and
stand, so close and yet far, often wondering when I would someday walk
down a chapel isle, wrapping in arm to arm a tradition of laughter,
good food and smiles, seeing one of your oldest siblings first and not
last, a generation of few still jumping the broom. Yes! And they say,
there is still hope.*

*The audacity you dared and desired for success and yet have it with a
taste of finesse, with eyes always watching, a niece and a nephew
always graced. This is strong heritage and much faith, passed down
from grandmamma. I think I hear her, much prayer and oil at night on
her knees that these somehow boys of her daughter would have favor
in their lives, even in the family line.
It's an amazing thing to be called blessed and truly more without
regress. I know that there has been stress with distress, should I be
proud, that I am. You are my uncle.*

*Uncle of mine you're like fine red wine, aged well in the right season
for such a time, the grape on the right vine you are divine. Picked by
God's hand. But I bet no one has ever told you how much you are loved
sincerely. We've spent much time using measuring sticks in all that
we've accumulated and still the love is there and shared from time to
time, through a dinner or a brunch, a phone call just to say hey! You
are our patriarch of this fine family, set and defined by the man that you
are to me. Uncle.*

Pride I have found to be rather pleasant at times. Often verbally speaking wonderful words of praise concerning you and, in the distance, the words have fallen on tenacious ears, finding refuge in the only real father figure that I truly can believe you represent all day every day, a real man. Embracing the thought that you have always been that to me, an example that men can be. Uncle.

Your life is testimony, real life, heart felt good news about men that are true to family and friends. I will write it again and again. Uncle.

If you've ever made mistakes, I wouldn't know. I see the glory of God in your eyes because it took time to become that in which you are. And if I were to never speak words again, I can write your song, I can play with your racket and I can even draw on this here paper.

I have prayed that I find the kind of man you are to me.
I respect you, care for you. You are dear to me, my mother's brother. I Love you Uncle and that's no lie.

God has smiled on the Men of our family and for that this has truly blessed me. Uncle.

©13 May 2008
Uncle

Soul Connected Christian

Hey! Haven't seen you in a while, a while, then again maybe it's because you've been hidden within, some kind of place.
A place where you think God can't reach you. Where you think God can't see you. Knowing you. Called you by name at birth, as a seed formed in the womb like a cocoon, ready to blossom and bloom.

Why cannot you understand that this place is not your home, you borrowed it when you volunteered to come, and He heard you say Yes. You said, I will Lord (Shout!)

What do you c? What do you get? But, with no regret. Could it be that you forget? Forget who you are. In him he died to redeem you, to free you. In you he bore you and, in the dirt, he formed you; put your spirit after he created your soul, created you whole, with one breathe into your nostrils, your heart beats to his voice, called breathe of life.

Life of creativity, for longevity, in you there is prosperity, for in nativity the Kingdom on earth to come, you are his and in you he refined you not decline you, gave you time, gave you freedom of will. Will you come and then find, in the depths of your pain, hurt, confusion and disparity, no clarity in you, finding you, disconnecting you.

You know....

I think, I think I met Him in a strange place, called lost and he found me at my lowest point on the road leading to nowhere. No where leading to mass destruction of self. Picked me up, dusted me off and re-planted flowers in me, and conditioned my mind with renewed thinking, presented gifts to me.

To change my frame of mind, like the way I think, the way I feel in control of my thoughts and emotions, feelings and pushing me, pushing me toward my destiny and the call upon my life.
For his life for his purpose and not my own...
Asking myself is this my home?
Home ....
Sounds like.

It nice to know that there's a feeling that is kind of good right now in a free-for-all kind of place called oops... not that Jesus stuff again. Yes! But do you like the natural high of isms? Realism like that favorite song you here from time to time, reflecting some peace of mind like that beat of the song that you hear you know, but no it's not like that. It's more like a new rhythm, new kind of walk on the fly, but he asks, can I have this dance? This is free, free to be soul connected and reflected, naturally connected to feel so right kind of itis in you, coming through.

He's bringing out the best in you and you and you like the most hidden parts, sealed kind of tight, locked up right, like pyramids in the night that I see in the sky staircases like that of Daniel's vision, Ezekiel kind of understanding somewhere in my id...Ideology of past and present technology, environmentally, sociologically. No, I am touching the Kingdom inside of me calling, me to purpose, purpose for being purpose for His Glory, Kingdom Glory.

©*2/2007*
Soul connected and reflected
SCR

An Evening Affaire

Starts with a dare,
Together time for two.

Romancing sweetness, caressing meekness and caught in a moment of
you.
Engaged, caught in a glance of rekindling a spark.

An evening affair with you.

A secret rendezvous of hearts set and then part, to a quiet room filled
of moonlight as candlelight, cuddling underneath a fire, a place,
warm and inviting.

An evening affaire for two, captivating you.

Compelling you, a destiny set for two.
Would you mind this dance?

No music, just the sound of your heartbeat against min and our
favorite song familiar to your ears, just us two.

©December 26, 2009
Evening affaire

I Bid to you, Anew and Fresh

It would seem as yesterday were here just today.
Looked upon faces a hundred times and never, knew this way.

I bid to you,
An engagement, a kiss, intimacy in the mist, lasting for a lifetime, still
the memory finds,
Loved shared.

It was today and today seemingly over and yet tomorrow,
Not far. I bid to you.
It would seem I have heard your voice before until afar,
Playing back on my memory, the recording so familiar.

It may seem it has been called déjàvu for two on another,
Rendezvous, looking for inspired hope of love to be found.
Painting a picture with chalky dry colors, in shades of green,
And blues, yes this is for you.

I bid to you.

It may seem that a new song comes to mind every time when,
You thought words not rehearsed seem to flow to
Easily and not apart, the words are concise and nice.

It may seem that you wish to know who I am dreaming a desire.
To finally rest, I know that Love has come to stay. The desire
I assure not far away, If you believe then your heart now knows
Its fate.

It may seem it were again yesterday and today is here again.
To bid you and I an enchanted fairytale of Love again new and
Found. Two shall dance the night into the heavens as the sky,
Will part and sounds of harps will play.

It would seem dearest and fairest of them all. Yes, it is you,
I have bid nay to thy heart; a kiss has been sent to you, my love.
A fondest of the treasures, I find. You have captured thy
Kind and true

I bid to you this day, a loving moment I wish to
Pray to share with you, my life.

© 1/3/98
I Bid You

Imagine That ....

Guess, what my explanation of drafting my story opposed to a song that you could hear often or maybe (mabe); it would seem better to let you really know where I'm coming from. I have never had anyone to share a life's story of their life, sit me down and just want to talk about this and that.

Find me out to just hear what is on my heart.
Cast a benevolent ray of care in the world or world and maybe that would be too much to understand that I do appreciate, appreciate the real, the real me and you that could possibly be for a long, long walks and talks for awhile. No, No one has ever told me that, that I could really feel a certain way or certain something's until now. I've been exposed not imposed to doing some things that's fun, spontaneous in a moment's glance and then some.

I ran with you on my mind all day and nite to think of letting you know that, in the openness of the heart, I say love. Is it real? Real to feel the truth in an ounce of your mind and thought of you. Thought of charismatic, spirit of an old lady on her way somewhere, somewhere to go and be to be, to be, be. Do not promise and deny your words. What? What kind of man would that be. A promise, a smile, a grin, laughter in the distance of a lover's heart?

Fragments leave trails of reminiscing through a heart that is fluttered with conversation that fills a schoolgirl into thinking things, thinking things like you and I could be in this for the long haul, somehow in a nice place where the old is left behind and the new holds and waits for us to see that...

The future is so bright that it blinds my eyes from the tears that fall out and down and out rolling down my check onto my lap where I catch few in my hand to see could it be? Howz' bout' that? Could you tell me the real deal of moonlight on sands of black and every handful catches pieces of your heart, mind, soul, and spirit? I'm talking love, a love that is felt running out of your mind kind-of-love.

We need a get-a-way or two.

I am down for going away on the weekend to see the world on a private jet or a car ride at that, and back to love, to care, to hold and feel renewed, refreshed, revived, and rekindled. Crazy fun and Crazy again to start all over again and again.

Much too soon to tell what this could be in the future but, I met you on park street, yea. Somewhere in Long Beach mabe Park Ave or mabe Broadway roaming around like you lost something, or did you? Crazy, I met you on the street, at the Lenox Mall in the ATL, at a conference, at the airport on my way on a business trip.
Crazy...
Meeting you again in my thoughts, dreams, and concept of the man of my dreams, most inquisitive imagination, who knew!

The thought that a one-line bar could mean I would be writing this in terms of finding the meaning to what I'm pouring out of my head into your hands; that your eyes can capture the thought of is she real? No joke.

The world of you and I that could be or is denied; is this what it means to figure it out or not like this? No hang up, just you and me. I'm almost there yet, in my eyes not seen to everyone, the utmost incredible thing that could happen, just happened to me. This time for keeps, this times something that I've never had before I'm not afraid.

It's important that you know that I belong to God, long before I belonged to anyone. Until then I will be here to do my task and help those who can't help themselves, to help make things better. No mystery. Religious No. Spirit filled? Yes! Not hard to comprehend that I believe in the good things that come, come from above high in the heavens, not seen to us in this life or world. Will we get there? Find it, in ourselves to know that God is near and is everywhere. Humm.

Sounds like, sounds like.

Spend the night? And let us get married? I can's say that you or I can be ready for the repercussion of too much reality that lives and is alive in the world to know that I'm just ready to be held, to feel safe and to be good to be a wife. Have we ever had a night to just hold? And wondered what the hey? That was not so bad at all the next day.

Because of you I want you to know it's alright to try me that way.

I'm a woman that can understand your need and be at a moments touch. Who knows what waits in the second that you come to a place where you've never been. Not afraid just ready to embrace it all and just to be, to be, in the nick of time, to come to a place where you have in mind. Time to be complete and fulfilled and everything after that is just someone to love. Imagine that!

Now, that's Love!

© 2/14/2004
Imagine that

Moonlight Bliss

The moonlight gives an epiphany to inspire,
Beyond the imagination.
Tears form resulting in joy, happiness.
Condemnation for the world, the world that,
Is crying out for more compassion, more Love, more salvation,
More the less there is a bittersweet of traveled roads,
Of mercy and grace, the mercy that waits and parts new.

And

Fresh breath of life every day, every day a new,
Lasting and yet short journey.
The silence is louder as the light from the moonlight fades into
Morning and the light grow brighter into day,
The stage fades as a bid to a long kiss with a slant smile
Of release to a Moonlight Bliss.

©March 3, 2009
Moonlight Bliss

Silhouette of Love

Silhouette of Love,
Still Loves here, right here with you.

Love is still here for you, to have and to hold, until death and life
untold.
To bear in mind all the years of fears,
Worth every moment of breath to take,
Such a beautiful masterpiece for two.

Listening to the music flowing down in streams of tears cried before I
knew you,
And before you knew me,
Listening to honest, integrity that silhouette is,
Hard working, kind, meek and gentle, you were then when we met.
And
Now you are my,

Silhouette.

A forecast shadowed through prayer; God hears.

Silhouette

Love is now and forever through the eyes of God,
In matrimony,
Love saw the woman and man formed faith as one.

Love is still dating all the time even through relentless time,
Through busy life corridors,
Causes growth, longevity,
In weathered storms.

Silhouette seen through mirrored reflections of our strength, in our
children.

Silhouette is "still the man."
More of the man today, you like me that way.

Silhouette is "still the woman."

More the woman today yet, the best parts of your heart,
Still captured by you and for us not far apart.

Silhouette empowers, inspired by God,
Ordained for the purpose of fulfillment in the earth,
By two,

Silhouette

'Still in Love' and more with you now
Then the day we met.

©June 21, 2007
Silhouette
Dedicated to 25 years – Renewal of Wedding Vows
Michael and Robyn Padilla

Sum Love Come Stay

Sum Love come around looking. Asked me had I seen her?
I simply replied, "Not in this time."
Sum Love say, "Well when you see her tell her I came by, and I'll return tomorrow."

I simply replied, "I'll do that".

Tomorrow come and the skies were blue, a warm summer breeze; good thoughts in mind, basking … in the notion of … sum love,
Sum Love come by again ask me this time … is she inside or outside somewhere?

I simply replied, "I did see her earlier and she told me to tell you… could you wait a few minutes longer?

Sum LOVE waited, waited.

I simply said, "Have you been waiting long?"
Sum Love said, "not just excited and nervous a bit."
I simply asked, "About what? Sum Love replied, "I waited and waited for most of this life – so waiting isn't so bad- I just hope she's ready.

I simply smiled and said, "Then I'm sure it will be worth it!

Eyes bright, smile cheek to cheek.
I looked up toward the heavens, "Praise you Father" you brought me my future and the desires of my heart!

Always on time and never a moment too soon,
Sum LOVE here to stay, never to go away.

© 2008 6 May
Revised 12/29/2009
Sum Love

Clap

Clap loudly.
Clap violently.
Clap vigorously.
Clap daily.

Clap.

Clap with praise on mind.
Clap with joy on heart.
Clap for the morning start.
Clap in the noon day.
Clap in the evening.

Clap.

Clap with Angels,
Clap with the Spirit,
Clap with the Kingdom,
To come, come.

Clap.

Clap in the mist of the storm,
Clap in the face of struggle,
Clap in the face of pain,
Clap in the face of the enemy,
Clap in all honesty.

Clap meekly.
Clap proudly.
Clap with eyes fixed on high,
Clap to break stride.
And
Clap for the Victory is already won!

©21-June-2010
Clap

Flowing Rivers

*He is the river and the lakes, that pour into oceans of seashores, he is
the sea running far, long and deep, deeper into the center core, of the
earth crust at his feet.*

*Motionless, timeless, standing before him, powerless, relentless am
defeat without, him countless measures of spirit-man roam to fall deep,
deep on knees praising his majesty.*

*Call upon the name like Hebrews that cherish his fervent power.
Behold! Behold! Jehovah, Elohim, Most High... Lion of Judah,
Angels sing. Honor and gleam, glory to the King, the God of all
knowing and all true being.*

*Oh King! Behold he that knows these names, calls them by the living,
Spirit and summons hearts to hearken toward altars, the altar of
First fruits.*

*It is offering time, the offering that pleases the Lord of sentiment and
Refuge in him you are found.*

*Enter the house of holies, holy, holy is the ground we walk upon.
Enter with admiration, adornment, and unspeakable joy.*

*Justice is one of his names that follows divine, divine appointment time,
On bended knees do pray, cry, weep, and with moans so, so, deep.
Understanding to praise be to God for all he has done.*

To God be thy Glory and the power, forever and ever.

Amen.

©*2/7/09; 2/12/09*
Flow Rivers

Give Thanks

It is the heart to be smart and give thanks to all and everything you do.

In the smallest there is surely the greatest to be noticed and captured for the

Moment.

Give God the praise and let his love endureth in all things. Exalt his Holy name on high.

Let us give thanks!

©10/13/89
Give Thanks

GRATEFUL

Feeling the heartbeat against the bed that echoes surging blood through my head,
Every vein and muscle of this body, God is there.
Feeling the power of God's love evolving in the process,
Knowing that the power of that love transcends across
The fabric of our genetic code.

There cannot possibly be time wasted on small stuff,
Breathes of energy toward negative connotations and privy,
Too much to do in such little time to do it all,
So, thinking of the wall of Germany, let's chip away and
Then hammer through and be thankful.

Grateful for everything and all things that belong to God,
Grateful for the breath and the blood that runs through the veins, to muscles and veins,
Grateful for the smallest to the largest of life,
Grateful for today.
Because,
Today will only take care of today.

Grateful for knowing that God is nearby,
Grateful for knowing that God is here.
Grateful for knowing that God is.
Grateful for knowing that God's word is always,
Today, yesterday, and forever.

Amen.

© 15-June-2010
Grateful

Jubilee

Colossal of rain coming down my face,
Showering in the mist of the parade.
Feeling the laughter and smiles,
Feeling the hugs and snugs.

Caring for people that just care,
Without the stress or the mess in place of less.
Factoring and calculating the changes that are to come.
Hearts beating faster, like we've been on the run.
Dealing a hand that forces its way.
But
We are a people, united for a Kingdom today.

God chose you and God chose me.
Together we will accompany the victory,
Pray it forward and stand in Faith toward the mark,
The mark of accomplishing our task together for the higher calling.

Soon, there will be no clocks, no rushing to get and got.
No cell phones, televisions, movies distractions just the same.
Just joy, laugher, smiles, hugs, snugs, and plenty of love,
Enough love to last, and last.

Rainbow and Sunshine, summer, spring and fall,
All together for one greater cause.
No winter, no sorrow, no pain, and no refrain, no lame, no sickness, and
no disease.
All will bow, all will confess, the day of our Lord.
A season the year of our Lord,
Singing new songs, dancing new dances, clapping, stomping, jumping,
and leaping.
No end to the celebration, no end at all.

Colossal of sunrays beaming down and around our face,
Showering in the mist of the parade,
Filling up on laughter,
Filling up on hugs and snugs.

Filling up on God.

© ***15-June-2010***
Jubilee

Mimic Me Lord

Do you not know? Have you not heard?
You are chosen this day and, on this hour, and you have just met purpose.
You have just made the 'A' list in aptitude for accelerating your life today!

Next stop destiny.

Looking in the mirror this morning and smiled, standing strong healed and free.
Looking in the mirror at self, smiling and realize. I did not do this, so it must be God.

Smiling. Happy because life came through your nostrils today, opened extremities, sent blood through every part of your veins, first thing raises arms to heaven to say, "Praise You Father' for today!"

Next stop future.

Camouflaging laughter after crying, shying cause you lying to self' about what you did and what you not going to do. What is wrong with you?

Next stop faith.

Jester on the right side, posing like it's the left side and thinking this is right,
Telling stories that is about to bless,
Look at God, Look at God!

Next stop prosperity.

Makin' new plans today! Cause today, right now, and tomorrow that is how.
There will be a new assignment, a new task to complete.
No deceit because.

Next stop is complete.

So, looking in the mirror mimicking, looking at God looking at you and looking at me.

It's all of us.

© 1/22/2008
December 21, 2009
Mimic me Lord

Shout

Cover the hills with a blanket of love.
The rocks will cry and be heard above.
The trees will sway away reaching high.

Birds will chirp without hurt to a glorious day benign.
Be it love, be it love.
Redefining the day with praise is it loud let us pray.

A sonic bomb, shaking the earth with strength,
The shout will pierce, the shake is fierce.
Giving a joyous praise, giving a wonderful gift with amazement and
thanksgiving.

Cover the hills with a blanket of adornment,
Lift up holy hands toward heaven and give thanks,
And
Shout!

© December 29, 2009
Shout

Thankful

Thankful for the life given,
Thankful for the mercy shown,
Thankful for the grace granted,
Thankful.

Oh Lord, grateful for what you have done.
Grateful for the love extended.
Grateful in song to sing aloud,
Grateful.

Thankful to be grateful for all that goodness has in store,
For all those that believe and for the many more,
Things that goodness brings can be,
Thankful.

Oh God of Host, Holy, Holy God of all,
Thankfulness in the heart of man, who appreciates,
The gift you brought, thankfulness that a great God,
Could love, love the creation created,
Thankful.

Thankful to be grateful for the life given,
And thankful for the mercy shown,
Thankful for the grace granted to extend the love,
For life to live for God,

Thankful.

© October 5, 2009
Thankful

This is the time to Worship...

This is the time to worship, this is the time to worship you Lord.
This is the time and place where we come, bowing down before you,
Oh God. This is the time to worship you, Lord God and give thanks,
For all you have done and all that you are.

This is the time, Oh God; this is the time to praise,
To give thanks with all thy heart and all thy soul,
This is the time to open our hearts,
Praise with all our might, reach up to Heaven,
And cry with a loud cry, Abba Father.

This is the time.

This is time. This is the place to worship,
The Lord thy God with thanksgiving in our hearts,
This is time to glorify. This is the time to pour out,
And give unto the God that gives much in his infinite,
Power.

Come on, let's give him glory, give him praise, worship.
Worship, for the place where you stand to praise him is,
Holy, holy is the Lamb.
The holy of all, the God of Israel, the God of Abraham, Isaac, and
Jacob.
The God of the Davidic covenant to righteousness,
Come on, let us worship the Lord.

Oh, let us glorify his holy, holy name on high,
For this is the time and the place, let's take the time now,
Open, open our mouths and shout with a victory shout,
Elohim! Jehovah! King of King and Lord of Lord,
No other God before or after, the only one true living God.
He is God, the Great I Am, the Master of our lives.

Oh God! Sweetness like morning dew,
Jesus, Jesus!
Come on, let us worship.

Psalm 96:9
Psalm 29:2

©17-November-2009
This is the time
Worship & praise song

My Brother

My brother, my brother,
Where are thou for the sake of just asking.
What's really going on, running out of time?
Spending too many dimes on bad traits,
Characterizing perfections for girls gone badly,
Good girls cannot be good enough until you,
Get your mind right, not so uptight, come on stay in this fight, no easy
flights and disappearing because you can't handle this or that.

My brother, my brother,
It is time to be true, sisters need you.
Be honest, be real, be the raw deal of steal,
Looking to grab a few keep them before God.
Praying all the time that you staying wise,
Spending too much on nothing, you've been demised by lies and deceit.

My brother, my brother,
What do you need to get you where you need to go?
Catching the wrong escape in places to defiled to say, showing pride in
a twisted fate, come on get your purpose straight. Coming to crossroads
that intersect to confusion, allusion feeling like conclusion to your case,
calling it a rap, while she was on your lap, rescuing you from bad
karma, it is called drama.
Getting you caught up heading for trauma, Cedar Sinai waits.

My brother, my brother,
There is love in the heart been tainted, fainted to your fears now there's
just tear; rolling down your cheeks, taking deep breathes of so many
mistakes and it's okay, you're not going astray. We got you. Hold on!

My brother, my brother,
We are praying for just a little while longer growing stronger for you,
Sisters' need you.

Brotha'

© **July 29, 2010**
My brother

Planet called Earth

Impress new creativity of ideas that flourish in bright young minds, minds of old; paint picture perfect watercolors in array of yellow and oranges so, that the world can see its outline.

No response needed.

Casual conversations of worry for a world unknown, unkind and, uncontrolled.
Let new freshness evolve into blessings that won't impose.
Let it speak for itself in an environment that resembles the earth in a state of beauty.

Show a glimpse into a new Heaven that portrays a still and quiet sanctuary for that, in which we were called, to rule in a sovereign state mandated by God; avenues that were never used or defiled by the hand of man.

Show...

Solitude, still shots of red roses created from love, hope...
A hope to nations, people, and children.

Pray people, Pray with fervent demeanor not apprehension,
A plan purposed from the spirit that created our being into existence.
Pray people ... pray!

Let us show the way, in patience, understanding, knowledge and wisdom shared from above and a grace that abounds much more than deserved.

Impress upon new minds eager to taste life with meaning profound,
The first to set painted picture-perfect watercolors in array of purple and violet so that, the world sees the outline of a new planet called earth.

Poets Unite

Who says poets are far and few?
Dead instead of resurrected,
Buried and tucked away for good safe keeping.

Poets save the day, when we stand on podiums,
For inaugurations, read by first ladies in quiet rooms.

Poets live on, filtering and hashing through,
Cultivated enriched literary art on walls of hallways and malls,
Explored in classic, conservative, and chic mosaic coffee Shoppes, so meek with
Aroma brewing caffeine or not.

Poets unite the spark of a new profound art piece to display,
Before the inspired, nostalgic, and hip of today.
Bobbing heads in dark smoke free rooms, do not trip, fainting to rhythmic jazz,
Ensemble playing, playing all night long.
One after the other marches on, dropping beats for many that delight, indulge and engage.

Poets for poetry sultry and deep,
Feel the air with language and no repeats of skill.
Teach one. Teach two or three, they are listening,
Intensely, holding on to catchy dangling past participles, verbs, and adjectives, which gives story after story, a picture, a song, a language heard of its own.

Understood by few, calling it a language a dew.
C'mon .... C'mon
Poets Unite on and on.

©23-September-2009
Language

At your Service

Humble thyself with humility to God above,
Humble thy knee and pray.
Humble thy presence to stay, for awhile...
And
Humble to serve humanity.
Set aside prides and serve all humankind is our customer.

©August 31, 2010
Service

Symphony of Life...

These strings are the rarest in sound, distinct in crowds,
Listening to cellos, violins, and violas.
Rare in a peculiar way,
Lovely catching the eye,
This symphony of life
You are God.

The Master lifted on high,
Majesty cannot be denied,
King of King, Lord of Lord,
Alpha and Omega, Beginning and the End,
Jehovah Raffa, Jehovah Jireh, Jehovah Nissi,
The names are you; you are the Symphony of Love.

Author of the book of life,
All powerful, all knowing,
Impressive you are, great is the King.
No one before or after to come, the only one true living God,
You are symphony,
You are God.

The celestial aligns, the galaxy refines,
The planets wait in line called.

The ocean calms on command, the sea roars quietly, lakes ripple less,
and streams hush.
You are Symphony of the Heavens and the Earth.
You are God.

©*July 14, 2010*
Revised July 29, 2010
Symphony of Life

The Hour

The hour is rushing nearby,
Can you hear?

The hour of Christ is nearby.
Can you fill it?

The hour of ripe fruit is being plucked.
Can you see it?

The hour is at hand, no man knows the hour of time, so keep praying...
keep praying.
The hour draws near, and time is few; so repent.

The clock ticks, the hand is winding faster than yesterday,
Keep watching, the days are shorter, and the sunlight fades soon.

The hand writes images and of the words in the frame of the sky; it
declares warnings and danger, so seek the word.

The hour calls upon a few good men.
Who will go?

Will you?

A cry of many heard in the earth and the earth reveals children and the
stains of iniquities. The cry of man reveals the bloodstained hands from
disobedience.
Who is to blame?
For all have fallen short of the glory of God,
And no one can "say, not me oh Lord.
Repent!

Who will stop the rain?
Who will stop the pouring inland, the snowing in the Mountains, the
sprinkling in the hills, the hailing in the desert and the sun in the
valleys?
Who will stop it? Not one.
Watch. Pray saints...
Watch and pray.

©4/27/1999
The Hour

The Latter ...

The latter of the two in what you choose or not ...
I would ask you take the latter of choosing between what to leave and
what to take keeping only what is light in weight.

I would bet that you take the fewer of all your worldly possessions,
taking what matters and what's at stake - yourselves.

There will be no time to make all the decisions,
There will be no time to carry it all,
There will be no time to pick and choose,
There will be no time.

©December 26, 2009
The Latter

The Writing on the Wall

If the writing could state, the essence of beauty that, I see in you.
I would not need a pen.

The writing on the wall has engraved your name upon its, rocky, dusty
platform, Craving a mystification of your thoughts.

If the writing could state, the charisma of fate over love, in one
saying, I would need, not to see but, to long the touch of you.

The writing on the wall states clearly that, I see you all day, all night
to say,
You are loved.

©3/07/1989
Writing on the wall

United

United by history, united in heritage and ancestry.
Stories of what was and what is, stories that connect fiber and fabric woven, connected, by streams and themes, traveled magnitude diagonally and horizontally, parallels of
Oceans and seashores with oars in deep waters.

In a future not far away at all, almost prophetic and beautifully orchestrated through, vision, interconnected not thru osmosis psychosis setting   in.
Generation to generation there's a gap, a seed of the new generation, the generation that was thought to be.
To be extinct perhaps even non-existent behind the shade of lighting speed.

We're connected like expected not tested for the rights that were the responsibility of you, you know the clichés of Negro spirituals, gospels of new and Old Testament the one that, acronyms stand for KJV. The one grand mom read on your way to bed and not. The grand mom that read, prayed, and cried out the word spoken, the lines of the perfect prayer. Though grand mom did not see nor heard, she believed with faith, real faith, the kind that produced the mustard seed faith.

Yes, you and I are connected through the sweat of backs that stood in hot sun rays beaming, beaming down on brown and molasses backs, in the heat of day, and night they rested; to start again and again and again... Yes, you and I are connected across boundaries near and far, that line connected to a brown line, yellow line, a red line connected to the black line, black lines reaching far to the green line that olive brings, that connect to the white lines seen often and heard always.

What? What does it say?

It says interconnected by DNA and RNA, twisted in spiral chains forming self-replicating genetics responsible for bonds beyond understanding, creating heredity links, building characters of inheritance. Shoulder-to-shoulder, we stand, you stand, and I stand, one eye blue, gray, some brown and green and the ones that you can see.

*Yes, we're connected by one, two and three or more ancestry lines, the
lines of stories told, a story too old and sometime just bold enough to
run that way for years.*

© 1/24/09
United

Where I go

Where I go you cannot follow.
Where I go you can't see.
Where I stand you can only watch and when I go you must continue,
complete the task ahead.

When I go let me know beforehand, that you cared and show me rather
than buy me.
No purchased gifts, flowers that go stiff and candy that hardens after a
while. It's appreciated and not taken lightly but, there is so much more.

When I tell you I Love You, I mean it and I tell you the truth.
All I want is to know that you Love me too.
So, care for me, ravish me, adorn me, laugh with me, cry, sing, run,
jump, and dance with me. Do it now! While I am still here.

Because time lapses soon enough; to not be able to count and realize
that time, just slips through our fingertips and tears won't be enough,
not even words.
Just pictures and memories of the life shared from a far.

So, sing a favorite song, one that you can see me move my feet to, and
move my head to and clap my hands to, a song that's filled with God's
Love, a praise song filled with praise, a song filled with life, a song
filled with the anointing of the spirit of God.

Lift your head and smile with me, lift your eyes where they can see and
continue to watch and pray for, he comes quickly in the twinkling of an
eye. Remember everything matters with God.

© July 7, 2009
Where I go

Vapors

Dust-to– dust, ashes–to-crust, returning to we must.
Sprinkled thin debris in the wind blow from afar,
Returning to the ground that formed,
Created by sculptured hands, fine tuning at his command, returning to
The meaning of life.

Formed from the breath and power of words that brought into being,
The life of mankind holds mysteries, history confined in God's eyes.

God calls to the spirit that is how he knows, watches,
Understanding the heart still grows.

Vapors are we…

Returning to the nature from where he formed me,
Fibers of dry sand and clay, smallest fibers of grain lay,
Questing for un-surmountable answers and the knowledge within for
majestic power of the King.

Borrowed for a brief time in prevailing on one journey,
Given as seed, watered for growth in his hour.

©July 7, 2009
Vapors

Printed by Libri Plureos GmbH in Hamburg,
Germany